FOUR SECONDS

a collection of poems

ALLY DRIES

CONTENTS

COMPOSED AND COMPOSING.

It's the way we bury crosses in the mouths of fallen lovers,
      the cool bite of cedar, wanting and waiting.
It's the way we build our battlefields on uneven ground,
      tide lapping at your ankles, a dog with a bone,
      cavalry conquering sandcastles.
It's the way we hold each other like parasites,
      like Paradise, like a plate of sunflower seeds.

Before the end comes the centre.
Before the fall comes the tightening.
Before the comfort comes the consequence.

There is only ritual and rehearsal,
the falcon and his hood.

COVENANT.

Just this once, would you tell me the truth?
Turn the stove off. Bury the eggshells. We've done this all before.
Tell me a story instead.
The king is the martyr is the hero is the orange hiding under the peel.
You have your characters, now give me a plot.
Just tell me a story,
where the crickets ride dragons and the ending is a covenant.
Reaching out,
opening your chest like a pomegranate.
I am trying to reach you,
but my knuckles are in the freezer and
your head is on someone else's shoulders.

SACRAMENT AND SACRIFICE.

Teach me about holiness. Remember to define your terms.
It starts with a body [a body of knowledge
                            a body of water
                            your body in mine]
Keep it simple so I don't get lost. The ground beneath your boots.
The blood on your hands. The milk in your eyes. Take these things and arrange them for me.

Teach me about loneliness. Remember to use my terms.
It starts with a feeling [a tooth in your gut
                            a pain in your ribs
                            your nails in the dirt]
Keep it simple. I am lost. Go on, open my throat and I'll sing you a ballad.
The blood is on your hands. Salt poured in holy eyes. Take these things away from me.

PLANTING SEASON.

My old head is losing its teeth.
                                    "These circumstances make better men," you're
reminded.   I am singing to you, tucked under the vegetable garden. Hands thick
with soil, hands that dig and hands that   bury. And now here you are, kneeling
in this gutted field,   forgetting your own history.

                                                      Circumstances fester,
pockets grow hungry. I am calling your name, soundless,   concrete. Urgent hands,
laughter   snatched from the lips of   giddy flowers.
A lesson you never learned,   "You're supposed to grow from this,"
                changing is part of the game.

VACANT BY DESIGN.

Your body feels heavy because it is not your body.
The dinner bell has been ringing for days,
will somebody please make it stop?
I am trying to warn you about the ghosts between my eyes:
                    don't lean in too close, don't blink twice.
Someone left their coat on the dresser so it's mine now.
This is called friendship: I take you and I make you mine,
          mine to hang on the wall and wear when I get cold.

Your body feels heavy because it is not your body. Not yet.
Drawing you close to me. Drawing you in red ink
on my thigh, on old receipts, on letters I'll write but never send.

+ + +

Think of a corpse. Good, this is your friend now.
Now think of a mountain. Something pretty, something to show the wife when
you get home, something to press behind glass and hang on the mantel.
Think of a movie. Any movie. No, try again. Your friend is getting cold.
Maybe this was something once. These four walls could have been called a room.
If you close your eyes all fire feels the same. If you close your eyes.
Maybe you're here and I'm not. Maybe this corpse is a sunflower field. Maybe
your friend is a room. In. Something pretty, something to show the wife when
you get home. You're doing this all wrong. Try again.
Think of a sunset. Not another fucking sunset. Think of your mother and tell me
a story. Any story. Good, this is your story now.

A LESSON IN BOUNDARIES.

A boy is a belt loop,
        a broken casket,
        a basket of nails for his high school chalkboard.

You are staring at him but he is staring at the grass.
"That's what they don't ever tell you," he says,
                        "it's more fun to watch the grass die."

As you grow older
you watch
your hair become shorter,
photographs as cycles of life,
                working backwards,
                watching grass die.

You tell yourself that
a girl is an anchor,
        a hope chest,
        a pair of pink shoes,
but the boy with the muddy eyes and the chipped tooth
made your stomach-ache feel like strawberries,
and for the first time your chest was a doorway
instead of just lead.

You are staring at his belt loop,
knees on the bathroom counter,
listening to his gospel:

"It's more fun to watch yourself grow," he says.

A boy is a buzz cut,
        a lavender bouquet,
        a feeling in your bones.

"That's what they don't ever tell you."

INSTINCT.

Like the deer that insists
upon the impact, leaning into the headlights,
I see danger and I call you

"mine"

A twitch to friendship.
A mutual exchange.
Be it the headlights or the prey,
stand next to me,
be my casualty.

TAXONOMY.

Name a thing and it's yours. This is called possession.
Name a thing and now it's a thing. Let it stand on its own.
Let's say we name a thing and it's real: now it can dream, now it can bleed.
Name a thing and watch it destroy itself.
Now you have a new name: casualty.

Name a thing and leave it in a nameless place.
It's a question of direction.
Name one direction and it'll walk in a circle: all things do, eventually.
Name two directions and now you have a problem.

Name a thing and now it means something.
Now everyone is paying attention.
Give a thing the power to name and call it a person.
                                        No, a poet.
                                        No, a priest.
Name a thing and let it kill you.
Now you have a suspect. Now you have a story.

MALCONTENT.

                            Haunt me still.
I am your creature. Open my mind's mouth and feed me candied sins.
I am your creature. I am reaching for you as you pull away.   Still here.
Shall I confess myself to you? Will you make me admit this too?
I am lured to you. Still, I am yours.   Leave it, leave it.
Doubting Tantalus,
How greedily I would eat you.
How greedy your mutt can be.   Now let me be simply honest.
I am yours to dispose of.
                                   Leave it, leave me
here, unrewarded,   baser than hawks and dogs.
Expectation breeds like rats. I am your creature, expect nothing less.

PERIPHERAL.

Try to put a name on every writhing thing under the Sun.
First, find your framework.
Start with a body. This is standard. Nothing can be new.
What's in a body?   *A pile of broken bones, burning.*
The liver helps with living, the brain encourages dying.
Knowledge is stored in the foot.
                Desire, the ankle.
Pain cannot be stored, caressed, or contained.
It can only be measured.
Think about it,
how we sort pain into piles,
        bodies into graves.
 I thought by now we'd have a name for this.

WITNESS.

Look outside. The streets have been emptied.
Look down. Your shoes are on the wrong feet again.
A complication for later. For now, look up.
Give your eyes to me. Look again.
The window should be clean enough to see the birds now,
I spent all day out in the cold.
The streets have been emptied. It should have been raining.
Maybe then this story would make sense.
You open your mouth and sparrows fall out,
                    tripping over each other,
                    feathers too slick to fly.
Look inside, the kitchen is swelling with birds now.
Look at this mess you've made.

UNFORTUNATE.

You cannot make a memory without making a bargain,
a promise to tolerate   the sting of recognition.
Memory is bloodthirsty,   never sweet without the bitter.
Memory is a room with one window and no door.
It is body: raw and tender, your memory sits as a wound.
I remember you in symptoms.
I remember you when it hurts,
when
the vomit of your love gets caught on my clothes.

ACTS OF SERVICE.

Which bird do I have to kill? And how do you like your tea?
Don't pretend that I can't see the rocks you slip into your pockets.
This is more than just a pattern.

No one is ever going to want you
if you can't cage your rustic.
Dig your roots out of the soil, the landscape can forgive itself.

No one is ever going to want you
with the future lodged in your throat.
Loosen up.

They say that tired men tell the best tales,
or maybe just the most convincing.

No one is ever going to want you
with those Caravaggio eyes, boy.
Grow up,
I'll be waiting out back,
a familiar ride to a place you could call
home,   or maybe
home enough.

OFFERING.

No more dead land.
No more empty light, morning sun drawn and quartered.
Clever thing, suddenly this pattern has a name:
lips on teeth, teeth on throat, throat on the butcher's block.

Taking your body and dividing the spoils in separate piles.
It's a compromise,
            a promise,
a division of labour, a labouring division.

Taking you out of the cupboard.
Taking you like Eucharist, a body inside my mouth, a mouth around a body.
Taking you home, leaving the lights on when I leave.

EXCUSE ME.

I didn't need him close, the proximity was never the problem.
Reaching out,
   reaching for him, if not to hold, then to practice my grip.
It's about building something: trust, strength, a house for us to
flood.   I didn't want him close,
        I just needed a hand, a prop for my demonstration.
Watch closely and repeat after me. No, you're doing it wrong. Tighten your grip,
        turn the tap once more. Good, the water is clean.
It's about filling something, shading in the edges until you see the whole picture.
It's filling your shoes with water so I can follow you home.   Please,
leave a trail for me.
           I promise I never wanted you close,
           I just needed a door to close behind me.
You must understand, the door can't close itself when I leave.
I would ask you to close it, but your head is already under the water.
 At some point this became a story about you. Did you notice?
 Were you paying attention? Don't worry about that now. Lean back,
I never wanted you close, I just needed to open your throat.

THE RACE.

A boy and his hands. A car and its radio. There's a warning here.
You will hear the crash before you feel the consequences.
A boy and his hands. A hand and its grip. This is how it goes.
You will look back on this and wonder.

Chasing History down the hallway.
You wanted evidence. You wanted advice.
But all he offered was this bag of apples.

> "Get out of the car," you said to the car.
> "Get out of my head," I said to my head.

Don't let this mean anything.
Of course, History was never meant to make us feel clean.
Who will remember us when so much has already been forgotten?
We unremembered, there is no shame in this.
Everyone wants to consider themselves among the martyrs that matter.

DISCIPLINE.

You're going to teach me a lesson now, aren't you?
        The history of unfinished races,
cardboard cathedrals, lining the roads with silver clovers.
        Something to remember: Philosophy is a broken body, just like yours.

Your heroes have been picked apart,
        something like roadkill, missing puzzle pieces, hair still stuck in the drain.
Your idols carved from old silicon and string,
        they've been segmented / fragmented / melted in the microwave.

I wanted to tell you my favourite parts,
        to wrap you in blue silk, to pull the bird out of the headlights,
but you aren't listening to me anymore,
        you're still drawing circles in chalk at the bottom of the swimming pool,
something like killing time.

I wanted to pull the car over, to tell you that this will mean something someday,
        that your body is my body is a bottle of white wine,
that History is just horses racing backwards. The history of unfinished races is just
        another body of knowledge,
something like Philosophy.

AUTOPSY.

The stage is wet.
Purple canvas
  stretched thin.
The stage is
groaning, slipping
further under the
sand.
Rose-red walls,
satin and sacrifice,
groaning under
the weight,
              under
the wet of the
stage.

Blood is
thicker than
water, but
dead blood is
thicker than
sand.

A LETTER TO GLORIA SAWAI, BRIDE OF CHRIST.

Only this day will be remembered.
Only this, the branches. The sour wine. The sweating wrists.   The pines, bowing.
Only the sandcastles, wet in their trenches.   Bulging, swaying, shells kissing the shore.
                    Only this will be remembered, kept,   carried in yawning palms.
Only this, the magpie shedding its skin, spitting up rocks through toothless gums.
You were smiling.
            Only, your smile was a bargain, a contract, an exchange for something more.
Only this, the magpie and his branches. You will remember this,   only
this.
            Spitting up wine, throwing yourself off the balcony. Only you will remember this.
A sudden breeze, hands stroking your swollen heels.   You are only this, skin and bones,
marble and vision.   Only
the artist.
Only you, and your pores, and me crawling inside of them. Hollow caves, dizzy wind,
            melting into your gums like bullets, like hot blood,   like the mint
tucked
under your tongue.
                        Only this.

CREMATION.

Hold yourself between my eyes.
Hold your breath.
Take my thumbs and unscrew them from my hands.
I want you to make me warm.
Set my body on fire,
I want to feel warm again.
Hold my head in your hands,
let me look at your eyes,
let me see you as you see yourself,
from the same angle.
In your arms we are the same height.
You'll have to lend me your shoulder,
I can no longer hold my head on my own.

PREPARE THE WAY.

Teach me to covet.
You caught me once again,
there,
       her hands, I was
watching them lean into the
shoulders of knives kissing
cutting boards,
dicing my lips with
the peppers.   Dirty,
a thing like that is, always
has been.

TRANSACTION.

Rosebud,
patron of the open casket,
meet me in my gravity death.
Be near me,   untangle my hair,
write your letters under my candlelight.
Please, come inside,
my tired soles are yours to tread.
Inheritance, donation,
a shift in the foundation.
Whatever this is, it's yours to keep.

SPECTATOR.

Oceans fold. We are
rounding out the clock now.
Doubling the reservoir, quick hands
pulling up fresh mud. Look,
I have seen your eyes in rear-view mirrors,
I watch the way you watch me, curious witness,
always searching for a new collision. Your eyes
collect tragedy   like
ants at a picnic,   obligatory, hungry.
It's only natural. Kiss the sand for me, I promise
to stay still while you look away.
You're getting pale again, stop slamming the car door.
Try standing up for your convictions with broken ankles.
Guilt is no easy thing, try it on first. See how it fits.

This world has no need for new authors of pain.

SWIMMING LESSONS.

"It's not enough to save someone drowning," you always told me,
                    "you have to teach them how to swim, so it sticks."
In the end you taught more people than you saved:

                    A man who can only swim with his eyes closed,
                    convinced that seeing the water will make you drown.
                    You taught him in the dark. His plane crashed into the ocean.

It was never about saving anyone,   I should have known that from the start.
You just wanted a reason to hold my head under the water. Let's call this a lesson on holding
your breath.   Are you listening yet?   Can you hear me
under there?

PRODIGAL.

Take your shoes off before you come inside,
footprints cannot help you here. Rainsoaked,
unlayer your sopping trunk, two arms stiff at
       your sides. Chin up, bare your pretty
teeth at me, your terror paring apples in the
sink, slipping slick green skins up your sleeve.
Remember to regret this.
                         Remember the ice
under the bottom step. Remember everything
that I taught you
last summer,
the backyard battlefields, bathing the red out
of your mulberry skin. Remember,
                    blood and berries
                    stain the same.

MONGREL.

Go
among the
honeysuckle,
scent him
out,
  find him
kneeling,
hiding coins behind
  his eyes.
Creep on vulgar
palms,
  chafing shins,
hound that you are.
Go to him,
paws pinched in
  silver shoes.
Tongue the dirt
from his wrists,
  the ground,
  the rocks
you
packed in his
pockets.

EATING ATLAS.

Burdened eyes,
the weight you carry.
Feel out his trunks,
hand under hand,
wrist him good, why don't you
frisk him up a bit?
Limping boy,
the weight you carry,
lend it to my shoulders,
my shins,
shed yourself
            for me.
Give me a show of it.
I would have you bleating and
beaten.
I would have you
quickly now, don't draw this out.
Break yourself down
into pieces I can chew,
swallow,
carry you in my
twitching throat.

PASSENGER.

You told me nothing scared you except dying alone.
I tried not to miss the train, I promise. I set four alarms
and my shoes were laid out the night before. It was too late.
I watched the train turn the corner and I knew I would break
my promise, again. I held your biggest fears in my hands and
fumbled the shot. It's my bad, really, honest, I'll tell your
mother in the hospital. It's my fault you died afraid. You
weren't supposed to be afraid of anything and I wasn't
supposed to be late. These things happen. These things
take time. Time that you didn't have. You're watching me now,
I can see your eyes in the mirror. You're judging me and I
can't even blame you. There are worms in the ground and
trains on the tracks. You could call this a conversation.
The point where the lines cross can be our conclusion. A story
should conclude somewhere, right? Oh, what would you know
about it? You're dead. I can see your eyes in the mirror from here.
Well, what do you know about it? That's what I thought.

FIDELITY.

Delicious crucifix.
A Kantian kiss
on the wrist.
Kidnap or capture,
 will you hold me down or carry
 me away?
Storing quail eggs in your cheeks
is   a sensitive game.
The sweat on Circe's arms,
hands that would bake bread
cracking omens into omelettes.
Exchanging rings with
          hesitant trees,
          coy and calculated.
I would give you my hands.
I would grovel at your shins,
               sputtering mutt.
I would bleed every berry
to fill your cup.
Gather the breadcrumbs,
let this trail burn cold.

TRIBUTARY.

            Wound in the Earth,
slicing into the skin of the hill,
easily undone.
Boasting tongue,
  charging on   leading
  the leopards and their armies,
  the dandelions dancing.
Look for the fracture, for the
pinecone priests with their swelling shins,
hear them sing,
            "He is coming. He is coming. He is."
You owe him this much, not a drop more.
Prepare the way,
 unwind the coil,
he will be here soon.
            Wound of the Earth,
pulling stones out of your pocket,
easily undone.

REVELATION.

From the citrus leaf
to the curve of your chin
      around clenching jaw.
Rare Eros,
        rooted seed
        in open wound:
craving cavern,
desire split down the middle.

A biting wind,
   bleeding plums pooling purple.
Rich and stained,
   bottled ships floating in the
   bathtub.

Wet pavement,
unplucked pear, seedless,
         seeking,
snatching juice from lovers' lips,
        a rescue, a robbery.

I wanted to tell you –
       – *"unsuspecting, do you think me"* –
over dinner, next time, over spiced wine
and candlelight, over poisoned pears
and porcelain plates, I wanted to tell you –
– *"Do you think me unsuspecting?"*

SEPARATE.

Think of yourself as already delivered.
The fields, think of the fields and the letters
we leave on them.   Think
of the ground before you dig it   up.
Think of this letter as a warning,
                              a prediction for
later.   Think of the fields, and the sting of
a love that only works on postcards. Think
of chairs weak in the knees,   of
affection without utility, how
                         lovely that might be.

CONSIDER THIS DEVOTION.

Write this down:

You are not the flowers. That shotgun will never be yours.
        Put down the cadaver and come to bed.

Put your hands inside a box and lose the key, toss it over your shoulder like salt.
        Lick your own wounds. Lick mine.

You told me that my life was in your hands,
I warned you not to stain the sheets.

It's cavalier, inviting.
It's throwing your shoes into the lake before they get too small.
It's something like a wasted investment, something like an offering.

It's about transparency. It's about driving the nail through the plywood.
It's the hammer and his constant questions:
        "Why does it hurt? Whose hand am I in anyways?"

You are not the flowers, you are a body in the ground.
You are an ache and you are a promise.
You are the lines in an old oak tree: a calling to count the seconds before it's too late.

Are you still with me?

EXCALIBUR DROWNING.

At the bottom of the lake you will find
that missing tricycle,
the one from the papers
with the yellow plastic handles.
The one from the papers,
the papers   you used to start the fire
under his porch.
Think of the headlines,   remember
the crumpled papers that painted your thumb
midnight blue.
Do it now, before they spot you here,
hunched on the banks of the lake,
the lake where you buried the yellow-handled tricycle
twenty years ago.
Drowning the evidence is no longer practical,
                    you wash what you cannot bury,
                    and bury what you forgot to burn.
At the bottom of the lake there should have been
a sword.

CRUSH.

The crown is foaming.
Call off the guards. It's over now.
Elbows on the kitchen table, lean in for me.
Listen,
Albion is black and blue. It's over now.
I am teaching you to kiss,
I am
pressing your forehead to the concrete,
                                    lean in for me.
Like this, here, let me show you.
The weight you let go and the weight you
will carry. For me, like this, let me show you.
Backing yourself against the door,
bruising your back with every stone I add.
Give me some fight, you promised me a show.
Go ahead, push back.

OBEDIENT.

Take me to you.
A sacrifice, a test of the will, digging riddles out of lions.
Tearing you apart on the mountain, on the subway, the impossibility of health.
Take me in, imprison me, bend the rib until it bleeds something sweet.

> *[out of the eater, something to eat*
> *out of the strong, something sweet]*

Take me apart,
batter my heart, sing hymns to the bees building homes in your chest.
It's a symbol. It's a sacrament. Butchering hands, consecrating the carcass you left
on the road, fruitful and forbidden. Have you gone too far again?

> It's an appeal to the audience, to anyone listening.
> Ruin me, make me new. Hold hands with my heartstrings and
> pull until the knots give way.

Take me home, I don't want to be in this story anymore.
Unquiet mind, your passion spent and spending.
Breathless, born. Needless, fall.

RITUAL AND RECITAL.

Devotion has always been a game.
Cat and mouse, martyr and glory.
Hunting for you in every lonely corner,
finding you
tying your wrists together,
clinging fingers growing numb,
an unfamiliar hand to hold.
Playing pretend,
pulling nails out of trees,
melting mountains under your
wagging tongue.
Playing to win,
victorious saint:
self-suffering for spoils,
poking holes in your open,
reaching palms,
rubbing your wounds
in cedar oil,
in reverence,
in soft-spoken Scripture.
"There is a price to pay," you tell yourself,
"There is a path to pave,"
but your head can only be severed
so many times.
Bread and life:
a bowl of water,
a skull caving in,
turning your body into a
pious tool, a
platter to serve
the Lord's Supper,
"Eat from me and you shall never go hungry."

Printed in Great Britain
by Amazon

13590750R00025